EPIC

Action and adventure collide in **EPIC**. Plunge into a universe of powerful beasts, hair-raising tales, and high-speed excitement. Astonishing explorations await. Can you handle it?

This edition first published in 2021 by Bellwether Media, Inc.

No part of this publication may be reproduced in whole or in part without written permission of the publisher. For information regarding permission, write to Bellwether Media, Inc., Attention: Permissions Department, 6012 Blue Circle Drive, Minnetonka, MN 55343.

Library of Congress Cataloging-in-Publication Data

LC record for Drones available at https://lccn.loc.gov/2019059258

Text copyright © 2021 by Bellwether Media, Inc. EPIC and associated logos are trademarks and/or registered trademarks of Bellwether Media, Inc.

Editor: Kieran Downs   Designer: Josh Brink

Printed in the United States of America, North Mankato, MN.

TABLE OF CONTENTS

RACING DAY	4
WHAT ARE DRONES?	6
HOW THEY WORK	8
HISTORY	12
TECHNOLOGY OF TOMORROW	16
GLOSSARY	22
TO LEARN MORE	23
INDEX	24

Racing Day

A group of drones takes off! They whizz through an **obstacle course** at 120 miles (193 kilometers) per hour.

The drones are flown by people on the ground. Who will win the race?

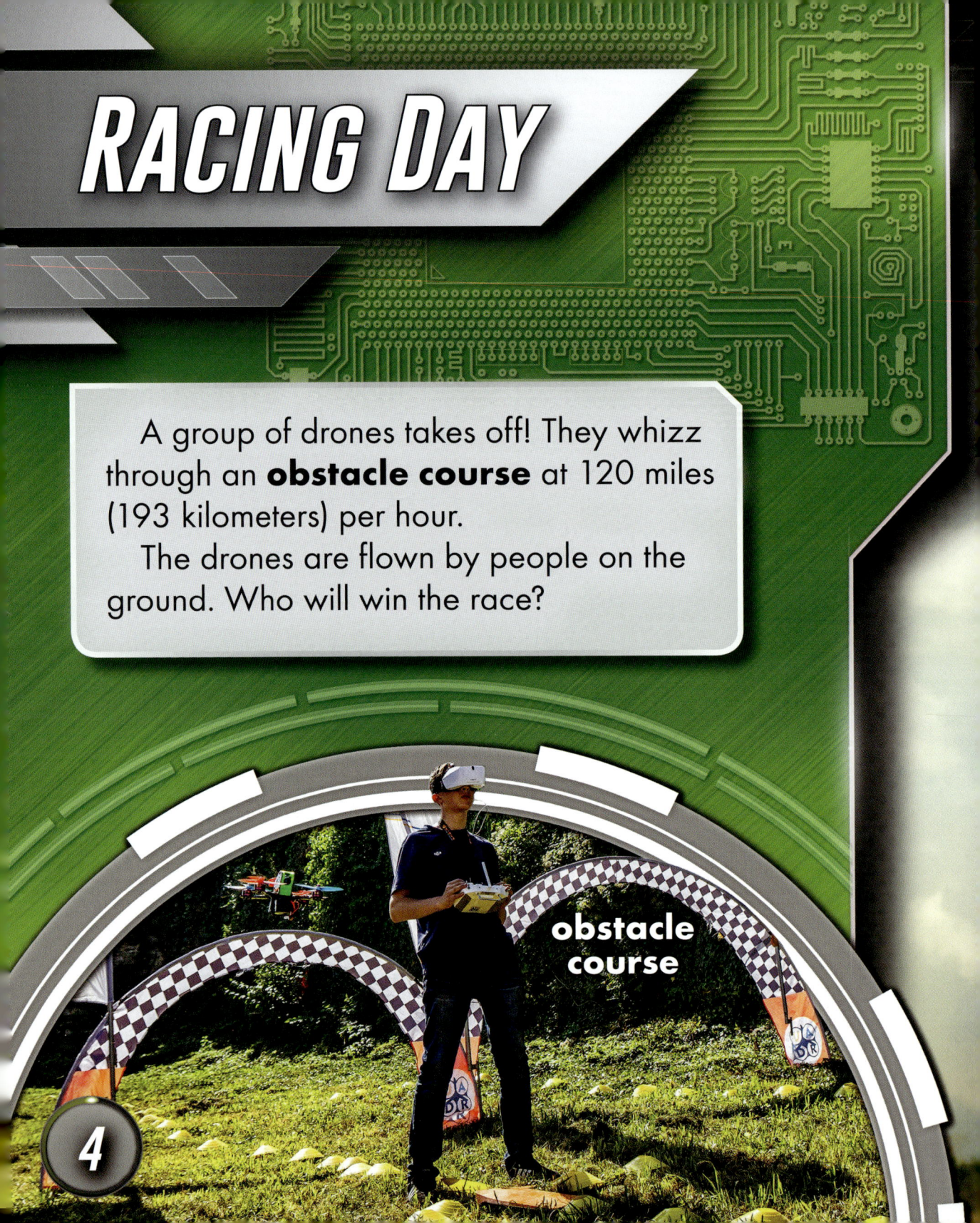

obstacle course

BIG WIN

In 2016, 15-year-old Luke Bannister won $250,000 for coming in first place in a race called the World Drone Prix!

What Are Drones?

Drones are **unmanned** aircraft. They are used for **surveillance** during war. They also carry bombs.

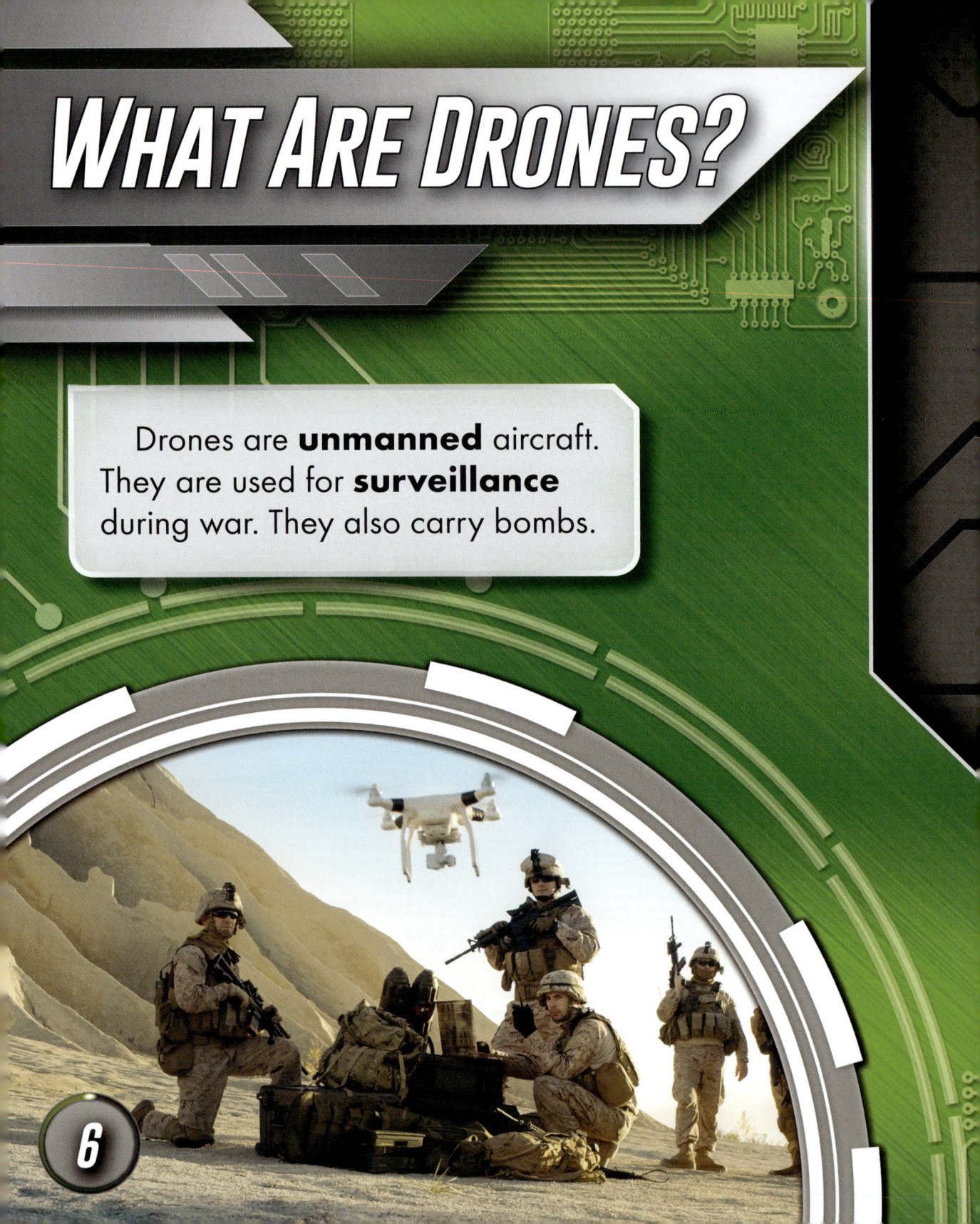

Who Uses Them?

rescue workers

filmmakers

soldiers

drone racers

Drones have other uses, too. Filmmakers use drones to make movies. Rescue workers use drones to find people!

How They Work

Pilots fly drones from the ground. They use **remote controls**.

The controls send **signals** using **Wi-Fi** or **radio waves**. A **receiver** on the drone gets the signals. It tells the drone where to fly!

remote control

Fixed-wing drones look like airplanes. Air moves under the wings to give **lift**. A **propeller** gives **thrust**.

Rotary drones are like helicopters. Multiple spinning propellers help them fly. Different propeller speeds make the drones turn and hover!

propeller

fixed-wing drone

How Drones Fly

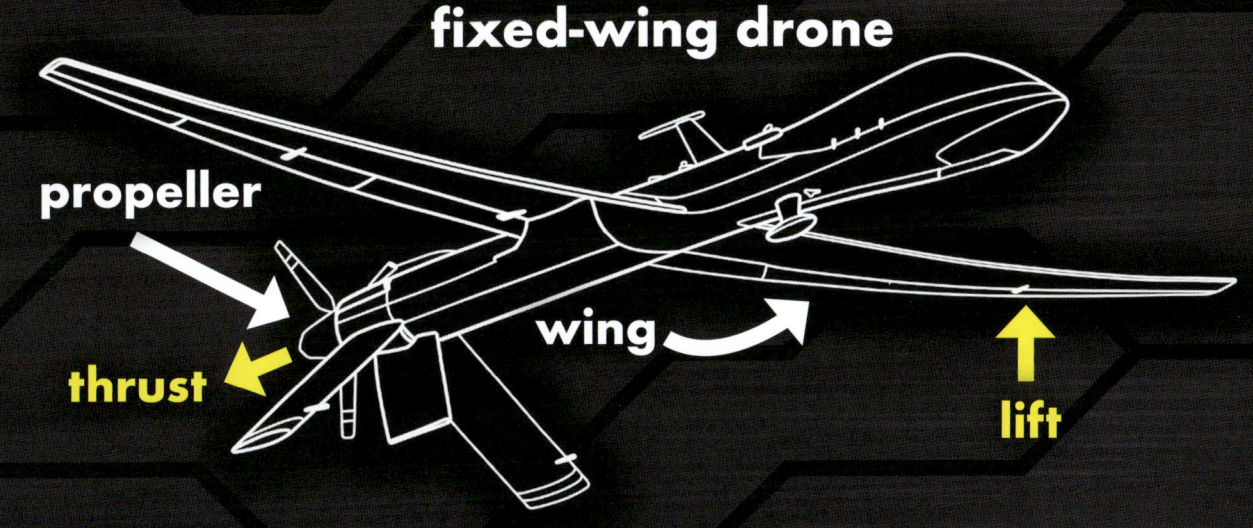

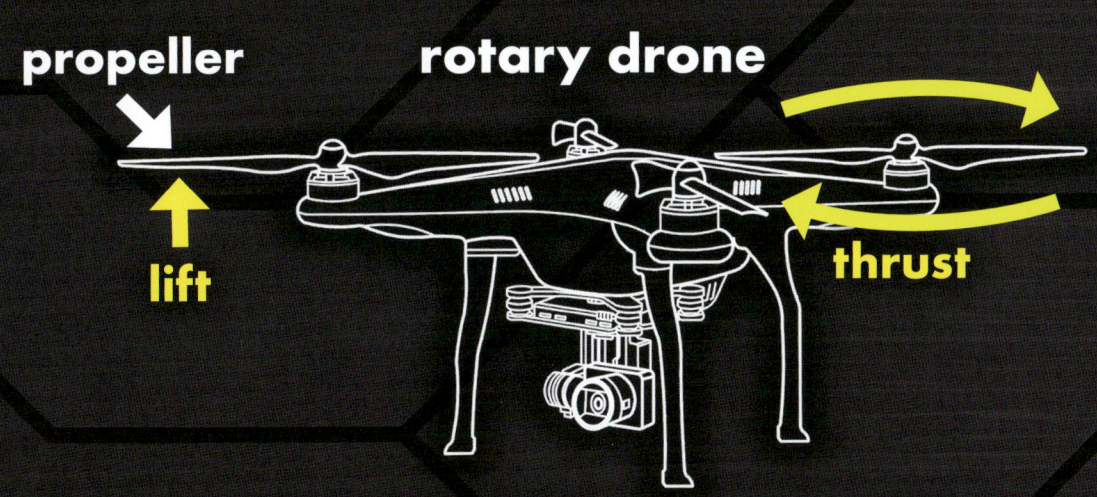

History

Drones were first used in war. In 1849, Austria sent unmanned hot-air balloons to attack Italy. Each balloon held a bomb!

About 70 years later, the first unmanned airplanes were used.

Hewitt-Sperry Automatic Airplane

BUG BOMB

The 1917 Kettering Bug was made to fly for a set time. Then, its engine would turn off. The Bug would fall to the ground and blow up!

• • • Kettering Bug

Drone Timeline

1917

The Kettering Bug is first built

1940

The U.S. military starts using the Radioplane OQ2 drone

1973

The Tadiran Mastiff and IAI Scout are first used for surveillance

Later wars brought better drones. In the 1940s, the United States military bought the first **mass-produced** drones.

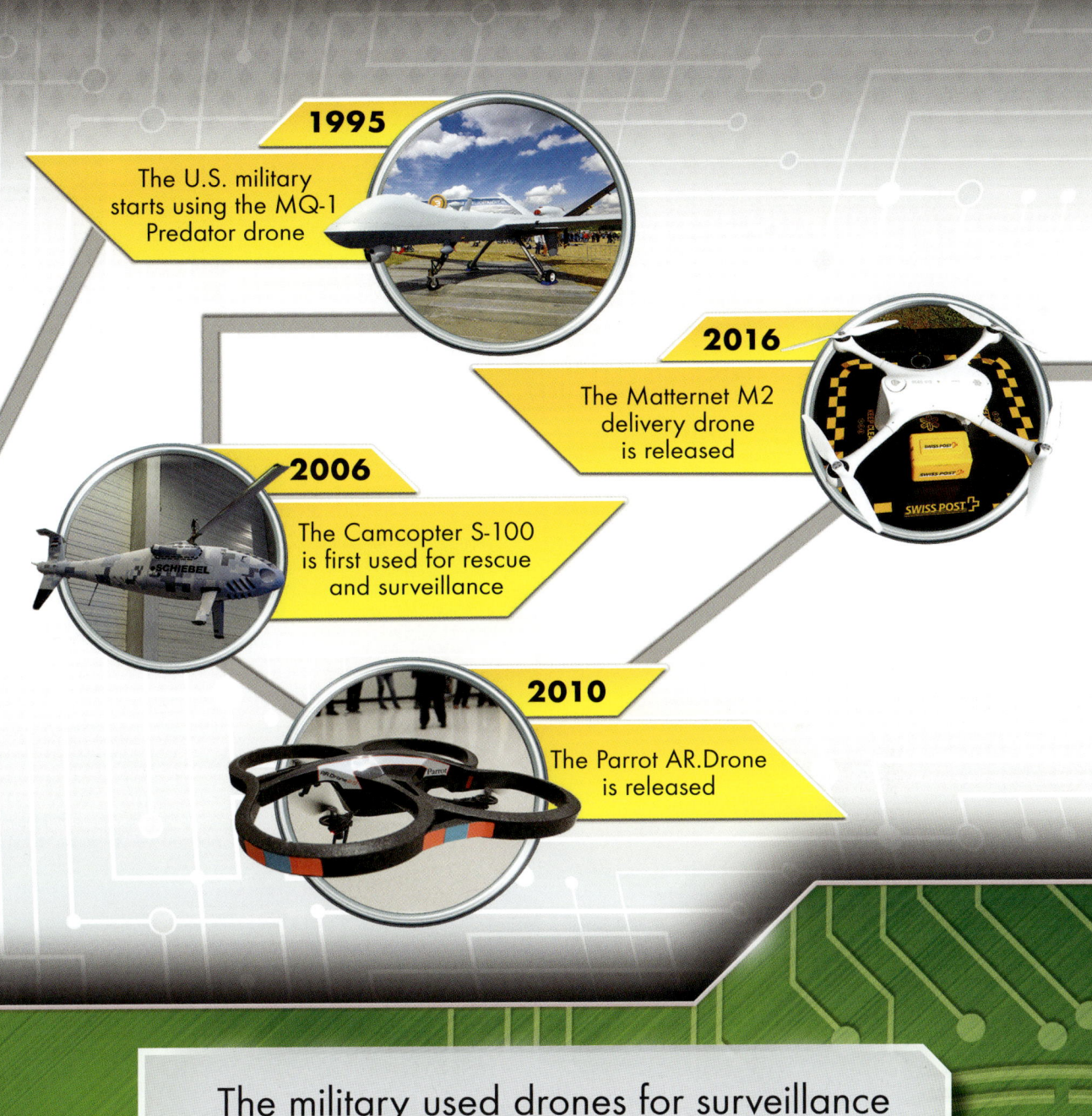

1995 The U.S. military starts using the MQ-1 Predator drone

2016 The Matternet M2 delivery drone is released

2006 The Camcopter S-100 is first used for rescue and surveillance

2010 The Parrot AR.Drone is released

The military used drones for surveillance and bombing throughout the 1900s. In 2016, the U.S. allowed companies to find other ways to use drones.

Technology of Tomorrow

Drones will continue to improve. Better cameras will help drones take better pictures.

camera

How Many Pilots?

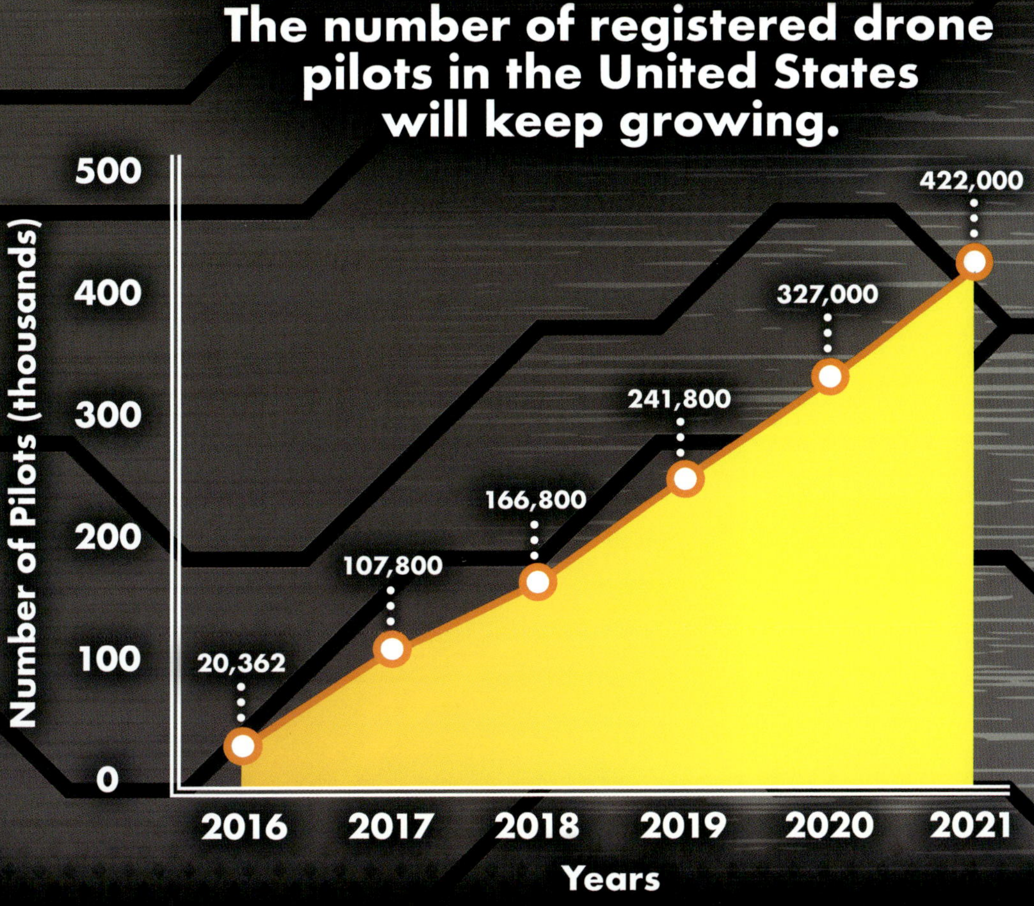

The number of registered drone pilots in the United States will keep growing.

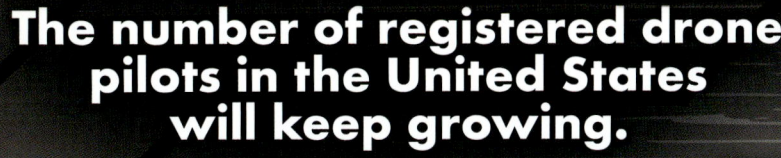

Number of Pilots (thousands) vs Years:
- 2016: 20,362
- 2017: 107,800
- 2018: 166,800
- 2019: 241,800
- 2020: 327,000
- 2021: 422,000

Motors will become smaller and more powerful. This will help drones fly longer and faster!

Future construction projects may use **3D printer** drones. They will print materials as they fly!

Drones may also be used for travel. Flying taxis may one day fill the skies!

flying taxi

Drones have many uses. But some people worry that drones will be used in harmful ways. They could take away **privacy**.

Drones may bring challenges. But these flying robots are changing the world!

Pros and Cons

Pros	Cons
 faster deliveries	 less privacy
 better research	 less air safety
 fun to fly	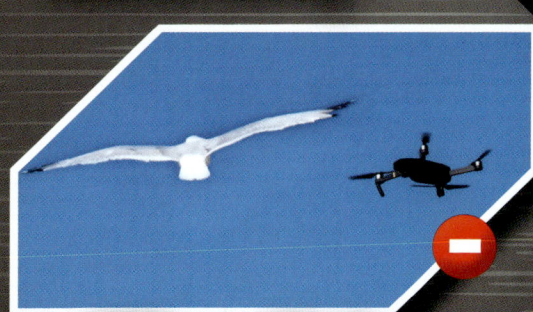 could harm birds

GLOSSARY

3D printer—a machine that uses layers of plastic to create objects

lift—moving air or wind that is used to go higher

mass-produced—made in great numbers

obstacle course—an area filled with barriers that racers must avoid

pilots—people who fly drones

privacy—the ability to keep apart or secret

propeller—a spinning part of drones that lets them move

radio waves—invisible waves that travel through the air to transmit information

receiver—a device that gets signals from a remote control and turns them into information

remote controls—devices that send signals to a drone

signals—acts that tell someone or something what to do

surveillance—the act of keeping close watch over someone or something

thrust—forward or upward push

unmanned—not carrying a person

Wi-Fi—a technology that allows computers to communicate wirelessly

To Learn More

AT THE LIBRARY

Lanier, Wendy Hinote. *Drones*. Lake Elmo, Minn.: Focus Readers, 2019.

Rose, Simon. *Agricultural Drones*. North Mankato, Minn.: Capstone, 2017.

Scott, Mairghread. *Robots and Drones: Past, Present, and Future*. New York, N.Y.: First Second, 2018.

ON THE WEB

FACTSURFER

Factsurfer.com gives you a safe, fun way to find more information.

1. Go to www.factsurfer.com.

2. Enter "drones" into the search box and click 🔍.

3. Select your book cover to see a list of related content.

INDEX

3D printer, 18
Austria, 12
Bannister, Luke, 5
bombs, 6, 12, 13, 15
cameras, 16
companies, 15
filmmakers, 7
fixed-wing drones, 10, 11
fly, 4, 8, 10, 11, 13, 17, 18, 20
flying taxis, 18, 19
history, 12, 13, 14, 15
hot-air balloons, 12
Italy, 12
Kettering Bug, 13
lift, 10
motors, 17
obstacle course, 4
pilots, 8, 17

privacy, 20
propeller, 10
pros and cons, 21
racing, 4, 5
radio waves, 8
receiver, 8
remote controls, 8
rescue, 7
rotary drones, 10, 11
signals, 8
surveillance, 6, 15
thrust, 10
timeline, 14-15
U.S. military, 14, 15
users, 7
war, 6, 12, 14
Wi-Fi, 8
wings, 10

The images in this book are reproduced through the courtesy of: Halfpoint, cover (hero); NiP STUDIO, CIP; Yanosh Nemesh, p. 4; BorneoJC James, p. 5; Gorodenkoff, p. 6; Mike Chapman, p. 7 (top left); Andrew McCandlish, p. 7 (top right); ProfyArt, p. 7 (bottom left); aerogondo2, p. 7 (bottom right); Michael Dechev, p. 8; Dmitry Kalinovsky, pp. 9, 18; Everett Historical, p. 10; stefanphotozemun, p. 11 (bottom); Molokotin, p. 11 (top); Kguirnela, p. 12; Niday Picture Library, p. 13; Valder137, p. 14 (top left); Bukvoed, p. 14 (bottom); Greg Goebel, p. 14 (top right); VanderWolf Images, p. 15 (top left); Sergey Kohl, p. 15 (middle left); ZUMA Press, p. 15 (bottom); ARND WIEGMANN, p. 15 (right); katuka, p. 16; agefotostock, p. 19; Levas, p. 20; Flystock, p. 21; Alexander Kolomietz, p. 21 (top right); MONOPOLY919, p. 21 (middle left); Stefano Garau, p. 21 (middle right); Ivanova Tetyana, p. 21 (middle left); Alexander Schedrov, p. 21 (bottom right).